DATE DUE

			PRINTED IN U.S.A.

LOOK AT
HAIR

First published in the USA by

Franklin Watts Inc
387 Park Avenue South
New York 10016

ISBN: 0-531-10616-0
Library of Congress
Catalog Card No: 88-50571

Design: David Bennett
Illustrations: Julia Osorno

Printed in Italy by G. Canale & C. S.p.A. Turin

The author and publisher would
like to thank the following people
for their participation in the
photography for this book:
Jessica Ratner, Arthur Jeffes, Lucy
Chapman, Coco Ndekekede, Yukari Sato,
Carly Martin, William Perry, Chloe
Thomson, Kate Tatum, Ursula Hageli
of the Royal Ballet, Leo Thomson,
Garry Studd,

Additional photographs:
Alan International School of
Hairdressing: page 10 (right);
Chris Fairclough: page 10 (left);
Sally and Richard Greenhill: pages 15, 16, 17;
Hutchinson Library: pages 7 (right), 13;
Richard Olivier, Select:
pages 14 (left), 18 (right and left);
Rex Features Ltd: pages 14 (right), 28;
Science Photos: page 9;
John Watney: page 22;
Zefa: pages 7 (left), 8, 10 (top right),
19, 21 (left and right), 25, 28

LOOK AT

HAIR

Ruth Thomson
Photography by Mike Galletly

FRANKLIN WATTS

London · New York · Sydney · Toronto

How different hair can be!
What is yours like?

Straight, wavy or crinkly?
Blonde, brown, red or black?
Short, shoulder length or long?

Babies are usually born
with very little, fine hair.
As they grow, their hair
becomes longer and thicker.

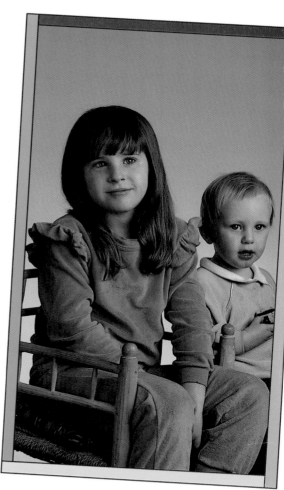

Hair grows all the time.
If you never cut it,
it would grow down to your waist
and eventually to your feet!

When people grow old,
their hair grows more slowly
and often turns white.
Some men lose most of their hair.
They become bald.

These are magnified strands
of hair.
Can you see how rough and scaly
they are?

Hair is one of the few parts
of the body that you can change
very easily.
It can be cut, dyed, curled,
straightened, tinted with color . . .

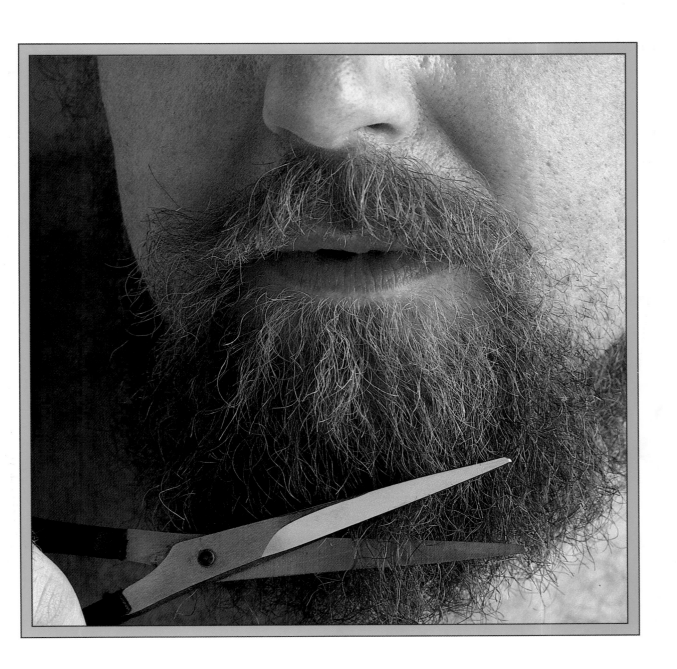

and trimmed into shape.

By changing your hairstyle,
you can change the way you look.

Hairstyles can be very simple or quite elaborate, like this one.

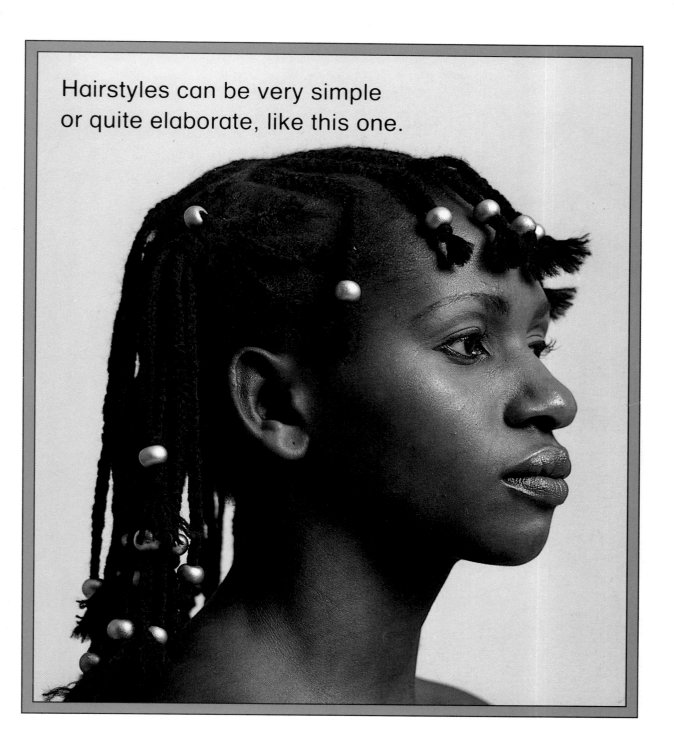

Sometimes people choose
a particular hairstyle to show
they are part of a certain group.

Some people have very long hair.
Others have very short hair.

Punks have very spiky hair.

The way that some people treat their hair shows
that they are followers of a certain religion.

Buddhist monks keep their heads
completely shaved.
This shows their humility.

Rastafarians never cut their hair.
This shows their respect for God.

Sikhs leave their hair uncut, but they cover it with a turban.

Christian nuns always cover their hair. Some of them shave their heads.

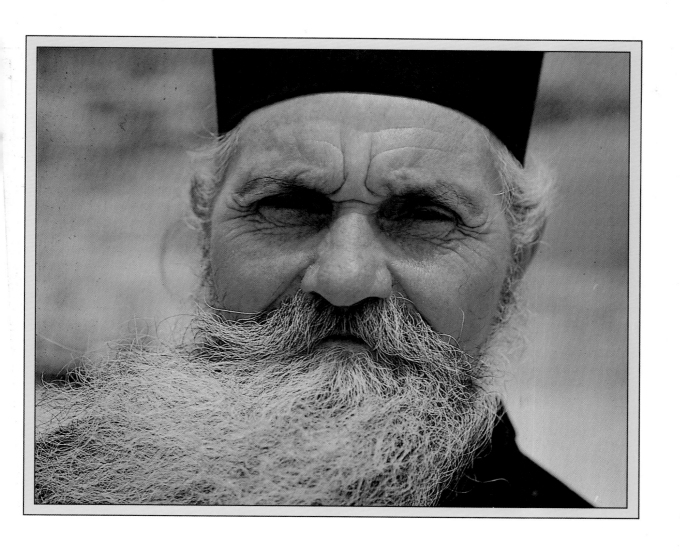

Greek Orthodox priests have both
long hair and long beards.

Some people have to wear their hair in a particular way for their work.

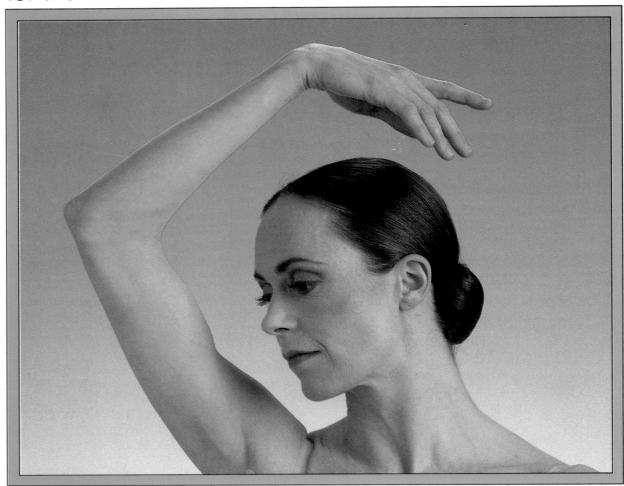

Ballet dancers pin their hair up
to keep it out of their eyes
when they spin round and round.

Why do you think surgeons and cooks cover their hair with caps like these?

Actors often need to change
their looks.
Wigs, false beards and
mustaches are useful
disguises.

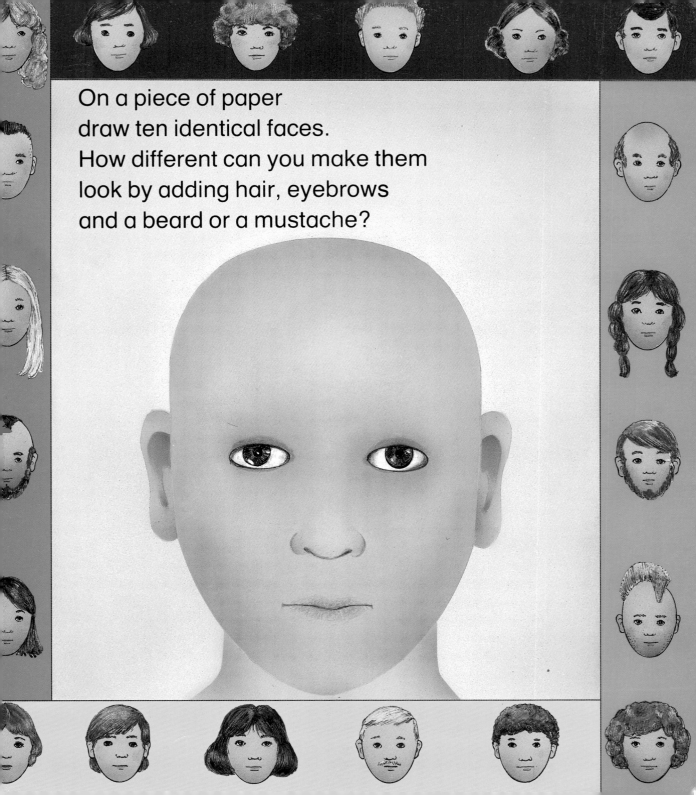

On a piece of paper
draw ten identical faces.
How different can you make them
look by adding hair, eyebrows
and a beard or a mustache?

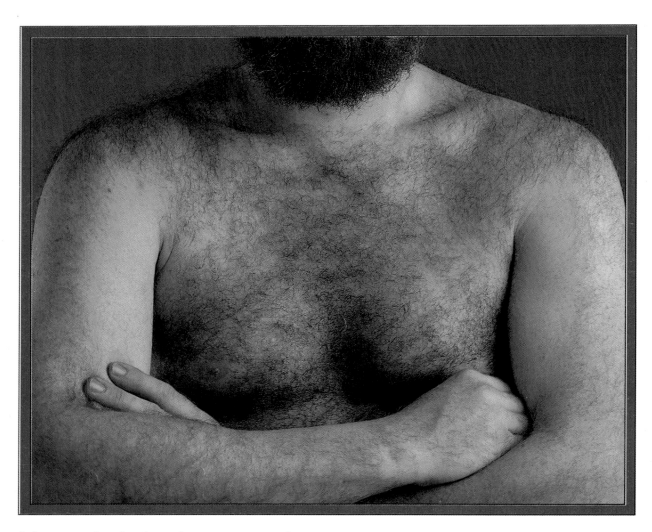

Your whole body, except for
your palms and soles, is covered
with fine hair.
Some people have more than others.

Your eyebrows prevent sweat
from running into your eyes.
Your eyelashes protect your
eyes from specks of dust.

When you grow up, hair will grow
under your arms and between your legs.
Men grow hair on their faces.
Some men shave.

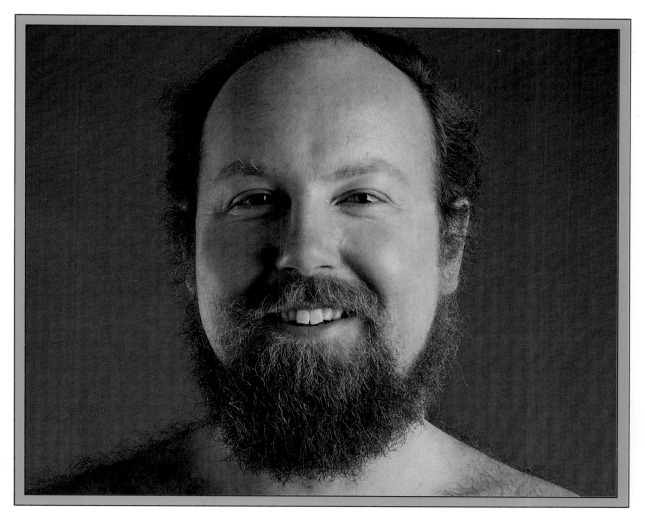

Other men prefer to let their hair
grow into a beard.
This hair is coarser than the hair
on their heads.

What difference would it make
if you had no hair at all?

Do you know?

● On the average, a human scalp has 100,000 hairs. Blonde people have about 150,000 hairs, brunettes have about 108,000 hairs and redheads only about 90,000. Blonde hair grows faster than brown hair.

● Hair is dead! Only the root of the hair (called the follicle) is living. It pushes the hair cells up through the skin.

If you pull out one of your hairs and look at it carefully, you can see the white follicle cells at one end.

● Each of your hairs has its own life cycle. Each hair grows without stopping for about 6 years. Then the follicle rests for several months and the hair eventually falls out.

At any one time 10% of your hairs are resting. On the average, you lose between 40 and 80 hairs every day.

● The rate at which your hair grows depends upon your age and the state of your health. It grows most quickly after an illness. It grows most slowly in old age, cold weather and during an illness.

On the average an adult's hair grows a tiny amount every day, amounting to about 5 inches per year.

● Hair is very strong. It can stretch by 25% before it breaks. A single hair can support a weight of 2½ pounds. If you weighed 160 pounds, you could hang from a cord made from only 1,000 of your hairs.

Things to do

● Make a hair survey of your class. Ask your friends to mount one of their hairs on a piece of paper or cardboard. Then arrange them either by length, color or from straight to curly. Make a block graph of your findings. What is the most common color of hair? Do more people have straight or curly hair?

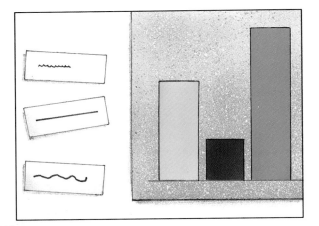

● Make a picture collection of different types of hairstyles. You could collect pictures of hairstyles from countries around the world, or perhaps you might like to make a collection of hairstyles of the past or the present. Write down anything you can find out about them.

● Find out the reasons why members of different religious groups wear their hair in particular ways.

Rastafarians, for example, follow a passage in The Bible, which says:

> *They shall not make baldness upon their head, neither shall they shave off the corner of their beard.*
> *Leviticus. Ch.21 v.5*

Buddhist monks, on the other hand, shave their heads as a sign of cleanliness and renunciation of the world. What about Sikhs, Christian nuns and monks, Hindus, Moslems and Orthodox Jews?

● Tear up some tissue paper into small pieces. Keep it nearby while you brush your hair without stopping for two minutes. When you stop, hold the brush close to your head.

Now brush it again as hard as you can and then hold the brush a few inches above the tissue pieces. What do you notice? Find out why this happens.

● Find out how strong your hair is. (You will need a hair at least 2½ inches long.) Measure the length of the hair and make a note of it.

Tape one end of the hair to a tabletop and tape a small weight to the other end. Wait five minutes and then measure the hair again. It will have stretched.

Add further weights and measure the hair again. Keep adding weights until the hair snaps.

What weight did it take? How much did it stretch?

● In the past, wigs were very important and fashionable. Can you find out who wore them and why and how people looked after them? Collect pictures of all sorts of wigs.

Words about hair

The word ·hair is used in many different ways. Can you find out what these words mean?

hair's breadth
hairline
hairpiece
hairshirt
haircloth
hairbrush
haircut
hairstreak
hair-raising
hairdressing

Sayings about hair

These are some sayings about hair. Can you find out what they mean?

To split hairs
To tear one's hair
To make one's hair stand on end
To let one's hair down
To get in one's hair
Not to turn a hair
To make one's hair curl

Index